Holistic Entrepreneur

Integrating the laws of the Kybalion into
the business world

JOSÉ-NICANOR PINILLA
BARCELONA

DEDICATION

To all entrepreneurs with soul, those who pursue their life purpose and their best version as a human being. To all those who try to change the world from the "unestablished", from within, without expecting anything, just by giving free rein to their ideas that will surely solve many problems in society.

Content

ACKNOWLEDGEMENTS

To the first entrepreneurs with whom I learned, Nicanor and Olga, my parents. To my sons, Joel and Noah, from whom I learn every day, they are my great teachers. And of course, to my travelling companion, my teacher and fairy, Miriam, my wife.

Introduction

It seems to be clear that the way to achieve excellence in an organisation is based on the beliefs of human beings, on their knowledge and previous experiences, on the established corporate culture. Therefore, the human team of a company must have, as a first step, integrated into their beliefs, as a driver of personal and organizational evolution, 360 degree excellence, a global vision and awareness, to act from individuality towards collective benefit.

The *holistic* concept *of Total Quality* refers to the fact that the culture of a company transmits to the whole organization a vision of continuous improvement as a learning path that leads to the satisfaction of everyone in the organization and the users in the market, as well as the feedback of the group in the organization.

Therefore, establishing a continuous improvement procedure, as something integrated in the individual and collectively in the organization, leads to a *holistic vision of excellence* in all aspects. In reality, it is an attitude that becomes an integrated culture in the organization.

In the holistic approach to quality, the individual aspects and the whole must be considered at the same time, that is the greatness of the holistic model. The only way to achieve total excellence in an organization is for the sum of the individualities (1+1) to be greater than 2. This is not understandable from a logical and Cartesian approach, as can be seen, we must deal with the subjective subtleties of the human being, which is precisely what gives value and the potential for distinction to an organization.

Whether it is a new start-up or an existing company deciding to move towards a more responsible and sustainable management model, managers need to be aware that Conscious Capitalism is not a break with the concept of capitalism. As Malcolm Forbes said, "*business was created to produce happiness, not to accumulate millions*".

To do this, as mentioned at the beginning, everything starts with thinking patterns that must be learned. These thought patterns must be implemented through techniques. These techniques and procedures generate individual and organization-wide habits that generate a certain business culture, which becomes a reality in the market.

All this transcends to the market and, if this "*holistic approach*" has been efficiently applied, the strength of this level of excellence in the quality of an organization becomes a "tsunami" in terms of the significance it can have.

Perfection is something difficult to achieve in life and we all tend to accept it. However, at a business level, it is possible to achieve it or come very close to it by following a series of parameters governed by the name of business excellence. Business excellence is the sum of outstanding performances in the management of a company to achieve the expected results. Through holistic we can enhance each of these interactions and make a more powerful and sustainable whole.

Holistic assumes that the properties of a system cannot be determined or explained as the sum of its components. In other words, the holistic considers that the whole system behaves in a different way than the sum of its parts. However, if we reach a level of synchrony in all interactions of all activities in the performance of quality in the company, we will achieve an "entity" that revolves in perfect harmony.

It is a new paradigm of Entrepreneurship, both of a worker on himself, and of the top management of an organization, as an entrepreneur who creates his micro-business. It is a new way of thinking (although it has always existed, but the market does not facilitate this model), of managing, of motivating oneself, it is not just a set of techniques and procedures.

It is to generate a *horizontal*, customer-oriented *organization*, focused on the human aspect of the members of the value chain of an economic and social system. This approach has the virtue of influencing the main value of quality management: the principles it advocates, such as the systemic approach of the organization, considering the interaction between all the activities and people in the company.

In short, it is not only about techniques and procedures, but also fundamentally about new patterns of thinking, a change of paradigm of how to understand the "*conceptual map*" of an organization. This would lead to a perfectly integrated structure with procedures that will achieve success in excellence and quality management, because it is already a quality organization, it is already "excellent" in the nature it is acquiring, thanks to a holistic paradigm shift in all areas of the organization, because it has already integrated expansive and sustainable beliefs over time.

The Holistic Business Perspective

The 21st century is considered the century of knowledge (Tünnerman, 2010), in this sense, UNESCO (2009) indicates that Business Organizations constitute a fundamental basis for the construction of the knowledge society. These institutions, in fulfilling their role, promote and strengthen the capacity to produce and disseminate knowledge through management activities, value creation, interaction between workers, and the generation of prosperity in society. They also promote the training of competitive professionals with social relevance.

A model is considered holistic, according to Salim, Yahya, Othman and Rashid (2007), when the model takes into account the integration of different perspectives: human, process and technology. In other words, a model that combines the human, organizational and technological approach. In conclusion, holism seeks to have a vision of totalities, instead of fragmentations, it is to see the whole of the factors that compose it, to see its totality, its complexity, to be able to appreciate its interactions, particularities, and processes, which are not regularly perceived if the aspects that make up the whole are studied separately. It requires a culture that facilitates the exchange of knowledge, that tries to motivate people to create, share and use knowledge, so that the organization gains long-term benefits and success (Oliver and Kandadi, 2006, p.8).

Knowledge management is defined as "*a set of processes that seek to manage the creation and dissemination of knowledge in order to achieve the organization's objectives*" (Lee and Yang, 2000, p.784). Likewise, KM consists of making available to all members of an institution, in an orderly, practical and effective way, in addition to the explicit knowledge, the totality of the particular, i.e. tacit, knowledge of each of the members of that institution that may be useful for the most intelligent and best functioning of the institution and the maximum development and growth of that institution (Del

Moral, 2008, p. 13). KM seeks, in an integrated approach, to identify, capture, codify, store, retrieve, disseminate, and create new knowledge assets in an organization. In other words, it is the way to process information to turn it into knowledge. Hence, the importance for organizations to manage both information and the processes that make knowledge management more fluid. According to Bustelo and Amarilla (2001), *without adequate information management, it is impossible to achieve* KM.

The concept of holism is clearly related to a vision of the whole, of the totality, therefore, we start from the assumption that this aspect is expected to be beneficial, advantageous for an entrepreneur. A broad vision of an idea or a project will provide a decisive tool for making strategic decisions in an organization.

In a more ontological sense, we analyze the thinking by which the characteristics of a being or a whole can only be known when they are considered and apprehended as a whole, in their totality, and not when each part of it is studied separately. Therefore, here we have one of the keys to transfer it to the business application in the sense that, in order to maintain the sustainability of an organization, all aspects of it must be permanently taken into account: each person, each department, each detail, and apply a group sense that gives meaning to the organization. Thus, an individual in an organization will be strongly determined by the whole of which he or she is a part; it is sufficient and necessary to know this whole to understand all the properties of the element or entity under study.

If we apply it to the human and social system itself, individuals are not passive vectors. The individual components are socially determined: society and a certain organization with a certain culture exert a certain power over the individual, sometimes even coercive, adopting rules as natural, when they are not. For example, trying to make life impossible for a co-worker, when this action has repercussions for the organization as a whole. According to Émile Durkheim, "*holism is opposed to individualism*".

In general, we could say that it is a concept that tries to spread a belief in a totality that exceeds individual human limitation. In a more holistic sense, we would conclude by saying that the synergy of the parts is more effective than the sum of the parts. The holistic approach is the basis of the holistic concept, where there is a consensus, and we can apply it as an integral strategic model in an organization.

Holistic as wisdom

"Western people have not increased their levels of happiness in the last 50 years. We are richer, we work less, we have more holidays, we travel more, we live longer, and we are healthier. But we are not happier. *This startling fact should be the starting point for much of our social science"*, Richard Layard, professor at the London School of Economics. I would add that our system is what it is, but there is no doubt that we are aware that it is "highly improbable". The holistic model pursues a common goal, individual and collective happiness.

In a business organization, under the prism of a holistic model, the same thing is pursued, in reality the company is one more node of society, which interacts with the others. The sum of all the nodes would become a whole, which would be the reflection of the reality we are creating.

We should ask ourselves the following questions, at least those of us who are directly involved in business, especially entrepreneurs. Economic science: what is its objective, how is it constructed, how does this discipline look at the human being? As far as the concept of wisdom is concerned, since holistics is very much related to the priority objective of understanding what is happening at a macro level, in order to be able to interact at a micro level. Where the questions of economics end, the questions of wisdom begin: how do human beings construct their preferences, is there a problem of mistaken identity, what is the common message of the different wisdom traditions? One still hears the following statements in a company: "I have one identity, one way of being at work, but then in my personal life I am someone else".

This split personality generates a real cancer in society. There is no belief that a business organization can be a place of learning and knowledge management, a place to share and generate all the potential we are capable of, to deploy all the talent, to have the opportunity to reach our best version, as a person and as a professional, which should be fully integrated. The holistic model does not distinguish between the individual person and the professional. The person is a complete entity that interacts with other beings to complement each other. We are not "lawyer", "businessman", "teacher". Our evolution as a species from an economic point of view and from the point of view of its levels of understanding or awareness we have reached great milestones to consider from the past in order to understand the present and begin to illuminate the future. This would also be one of the approaches of Holistics, to have a vision of what we have been, what we are, and what we may be capable of being.

On a practical and daily level, not growing in economic terms generates suffering (crisis and unemployment); however, economic growth leads to environmental deterioration that compromises the viability of the planet and the survival of the species itself (Valverde, 2017). In the case we are experiencing in 2020 with the pandemic, we can see the forcefulness and strength that globality has in the face of everyday life. Is there a plausible and realistic way out of this crossroads? What does traditional economic science tell us? How to approach the problem from Wisdom or from a Holistic approach? All these questions are necessary to understand that the solution to a problem is not done from the same mental parameters that generated the problem, but from a different perspective to create a different reality. At the individual or organizational level, this is not clear to them, they try to solve problems from the same mental parameters, the same paradigm, the same "conceptual framework". The holistic model has built in, in itself, the flexibility of different approaches "outside the box" and bringing together a consensus on different patterns of thinking that in the end, in a world of possibilities, the organization will find the best version of the solution for all and as an individual entity.

Is economic science moving us closer to or further away from the Wisdom/Holism proposals?

What should be our guide as we move forward into the uncertain future? Is reason - being rational - the ultimate goal of evolution in the economy and society? In times of uncertainty such as those we are currently experiencing due to the Covid-19 pandemic, the first thing that comes to mind is fear among the population and secondly, how I am going to survive. It is clear that, at a time of economic and financial crisis, the population is trying to find a new paradigm for subsistence. One of the characteristics of the holistic model is that it already contemplates the possibility of moments of uncertainty and paradigm shifts, given that the economy, like the current situation, is a constant and evolving process, sometimes expansive, sometimes contracting. We have been educated, in general, that if I stay as I am, things will go better. We can affirm today that any entrepreneur must be aware that there will be hard times, difficult trials to overcome, and that is part of the game, as well as times when everything will flow without any apparent effort. *"If you can see trials as opportunities, then the way you live your life is fine. Understand this and you will already know something great about living life"* (Inamori, K. 2009, p. 4).

Holistic as happiness

We can say that the conclusions drawn by Achor in his book "The Happiness Advantage", what happiness at work brings, are encouraging and surprising. One of his statements says that "*countless studies have found that social relationships are the best guarantee of increased well-being and decreased stress, both an antidote to depression and a recipe for high performance*". Therefore, from the paradigm of the holistic concept, it is perfectly aligned with understanding an organization as an entity where a group of people interact with each other. If in these relationships common goals are pursued and the common good is realized, performance levels soar. Because positive brains have a biological advantage over neutral or negative brains, the Happiness Advantage teaches us how to reprogram our brains to capitalize on positivity and improve our productivity and performance.

Of course, within the concept of holism, this is not a denial of negativism, nor is it a denial that at times there will be problems and lack of understanding. They are already seen as opportunities for improvement. When challenges loom and we feel overwhelmed, our rational brains can be hijacked by emotions. The Fox Circle (Achor, 2010) teaches us how to regain control by first focusing on small, manageable goals, and then gradually expanding our circle to achieve larger and larger ones.

Sustaining lasting change often feels impossible because our willpower is limited. And when willpower fails, we revert to our old habits and succumb to the path of least resistance. Organizations try to solve emerging problems under the same paradigm that created them, so it becomes a vicious cycle.

From the holistic point of view, solutions often appear from "out of the box" parameters, since it is understood that, in order to find solutions to new problems, we must do so from different perspectives of thought that were not being applied until then.

As a summary, we will provide an overview of the benefits of happiness (Achor, 2010):

✓ Happiness is not just a state of mind, it is a work ethic.

✓ We can use our brains to change the way we process the world, and that in turn changes the way we react to it.

✓ Constantly scanning the world for the positive allows us to experience happiness, gratitude and optimism.

✓ When we reframe failure as an opportunity for growth, we are more likely to experience that growth.

✓ The most successful people, in work and in life, believe that their actions have a direct effect on their results.

It is therefore clear that organizations need to implement policies and measures aimed at improving the satisfaction and motivation of human capital. While this idea is not new, and most employers are aware of the relationship between workforce happiness and productivity, the problem with the traditional system is that it neglected the drive for team wellbeing.

Holistic as education

Holistic education (from the Greek "holos", totality) was born in the 1990s and is undoubtedly the educational paradigm for the 21st century. It is based on the premise that each human being is unique and unrepeatable, but, at the same time, is intrinsically related to everything that surrounds him or her. In other words, each human being is a holon, a part of a hologram or totality, whose parts he or she contains. Holistic education is not an educational method, but a creative and holistic view of education. Within this research into the concept of holistic education, we can see that this model has been applied for years in the education sector.

For example, in the Montessori model, or in the Waldorf system. In the former, the Montessori classroom integrates age groups in 3-year periods, which naturally promotes socialization, respect and solidarity. In the Waldorf method, it is one of the educational systems that appears as an alternative to the traditional Prussian educational system. Waldorf pedagogy, initiated by the German philosopher Rudolf Steiner, seeks the development of each child in a free and cooperative environment, without examinations and with strong support for art and manual work, which results in a great sensitivity and awareness of the potential of each pupil, as well as a feeling of group.

We can identify, by analyzing various sources of holistic education, that it is an education for life, which contemplates the human being as a whole and not just as a brain, in which only the left hemisphere (the logical, analytical, rational) is appealed to the detriment of the right hemisphere (the intuitive, creative, imaginative). It is an education that goes beyond the cognitive aspect, it also focuses on the physical, emotional, and spiritual aspects to form a more integral being. Therefore, here again we are clear about the holistic concept, a vision of the whole, from the individuality.

Holistic education is a humanistic pedagogy centered on the student and interested, above all, in their formation and development as a person, in their relationship with themselves and, as a being in society, in their relationship with others and with the planet (Cabestany, 2018). In addition, it incorporates the secular spiritual aspect, which has not been considered by other pedagogical currents.

As knowledge of Higher Education, and as a prelude to the future entrepreneur, we note that most higher education institutions, given the serious unemployment we face in our society, accept that it is necessary to train young people to join the labour market, but very few focus on them being the creators of their own work.

It is a very laudable objective, but unfortunately it is not achieved in most cases, since many of them enter the productive activity as employees or underemployed and in the worst case to swell the unemployment rates; However, it is a fact that from the holistic education point of view, academic programs continue to provide a partial, materialistic training, so that future higher level graduates lack a comprehensive training, a training that allows them to evolve their consciousness and be happy in this human experience, facing uncertainty with self-confidence, truly developing creativity and successfully resolving the vicissitudes of the workplace and in particular of business as a conscious entrepreneur.

And above all, to establish in educational programs the evidence that entrepreneurship in any professional activity is possible, from an objective point of view, and furthermore, that it is seen as an alternative, not easy to achieve, although with a certain empowerment of students, it can be seen as a motivating and transforming way of life for society.

The essential purpose of education is to evolve the consciousness of the human being, and in the vision of holistic education one aspect is precisely that the human being evolves to higher levels of consciousness, so that ultimately the human being uses his full potential in the service of society and to experience his true essence, which is to be happy.

A conscious entrepreneur is happy and feels fully satisfied in his activity and learning path, serving society and therefore, himself, as Marci Shimoff puts it "*happiness has nothing to do with having everything you have dreamed of owning and it is not about simply denying the need for material comforts in this life. What we all really seek is happiness that comes from within and does not depend on external circumstances, the kind of happiness that I call happiness for its own sake*" (Shimoff, 2008).

Holistic Knowledge

Talent Management System Analysis in an Organization

Based on *conscious capitalism*, it is this work motivation that will lead to better employee performance and higher profitability, not vice versa. Conscious leaders prefer to have happy employees, even if this means lower profits for shareholders in the short term, because they know that, in the medium to long term, employee satisfaction will multiply the profits of all stakeholders, including investors.

To implement a talent management policy, employers need to be aware of what makes employees happy, what really motivates employees, i.e., from applying generalized, preconceived and, in some cases, outdated ideas about satisfaction to looking directly at the reasons of each employee that trigger their engagement.

During the 20th century, traditional capitalism has associated job satisfaction mainly with extrinsic factors, such as higher salaries or health insurance. Without undermining the importance of these elements in the motivation of professionals, today we know that the most important thing to create engaged teams is to respond to the intrinsic motivations of each worker, creating an emotional relationship of respect and trust between the company and the human capital that turns them into a single entity that moves in unison with a common purpose and values (SIDODIA; MACKEY, Conscious Capitalism, *2013*).

According to Reaich, Gemino and Sauer (2012) Knowledge Management should foster a social and technological environment that favours knowledge-related activities, to promote the creation, storage, and dissemination of knowledge. KM seeks, in an integrated approach, to identify, capture, codify, store, retrieve, disseminate, and create new knowledge assets in an organization. In other words, it is the way to process information to turn it into knowledge.

From the point of view of a holistic model, the aim is to facilitate the understanding and treatment of the complexity of systems. According to Sánchez (2005), a QA model *is a tool that allows a simplified, summarized, symbolic, schematic representation.* A model is considered holistic, according to Salim, Yahya, Othman and Rashid (2007), when the model takes into account the integration of different perspectives: human, processes and technology. That is, a model that combines human, organizational and technological approaches.

We can affirm in general, in order to carry out a holistic model in Knowledge Management and excellence in quality and performance, it is necessary to involve people, as this is where knowledge resides, that is, they are the ones who create knowledge and use it in their activity.

Therefore, in the organizational culture, in the mission and vision of the company, the conditions must be created to facilitate and encourage people so that the process of knowledge creation and transmission can be carried out in an appropriate way.

In other words, the processes allow production to be optimized, they are the keys to the organization, they represent the know-how in this context, in other words, they are the actions, as well as the unfolding of the tasks and functions of the organization, which are represented by administrative, organizational, technical, and operational management.

Information and communication technologies (ICT) are those that facilitate the management of communications, information, and knowledge through the efficient management of hardware (computers and communication networks) and software (systems and programs). Today our interaction is based on a digital environment. In the first instance it does not have to disintegrate communication between workers, it should be understood as a tool to be able to go further and manage time, optimize efforts and help to share horizontal information for all self-managed teams.

As Raj Sisodia and John Mackey state in their book "*Conscious Capitalism*", it is possible to "*build a company out of love and trust rather than fear and stress*", making employee satisfaction one of the fundamental pillars of such an activity. Realistically, society today is not ready for such a strategic approach, as most partners or employees in an organization would be perplexed by a corporate culture with such an approach. They would most likely think they were in a cult, rather than a business organization.

In conclusion, the holistic model for Knowledge Management and excellence seeks to have a vision of totalities, instead of fragmentations, to understand and comprehend a 360 degree vision, a whole set of the factors that compose it, to see its totality, its complexity, to be able to appreciate its interactions, particularities and processes, which are not regularly perceived if the aspects that make up the whole are studied separately. Let's see what the paradigm shift would be.

Holistic Model in Business Organizational Excellence: THE CONSCIOUS COMPANY

One of the first premises to consider is how to create a conscious company. Unlike traditional capitalism, the concern of conscious companies is not only focused on investors, but their mission is equally centered on all groups within the organization. The organization that wants to break into the market under the principles of Conscious Capitalism must assume that, by taking care of all stakeholders and satisfying their needs and demands, no interest group will have to make sacrifices for the benefit of another. This leads to the ultimate goal of organizational excellence.

In a company with a holistic model, due to a broad vision of the entire spectrum of the organization, all the agents involved in the interaction of all the processes back and forth are strengthened by the development of synergies and collaborations that enable joint progress towards the objectives.

It is obvious and necessary to ask ourselves again something that is vital to the survival of any business organization. We must ask ourselves about the profitability of implementing a *holistic model of excellence*. Why are conscious companies more profitable? As Raj Sisodia, David Wolfe and Jag Seth point out in their book Firms of Endearment, we are currently witnessing a change of mindset, what they call the *Age of Transcendence*, and it is precisely at times like these that new models of business excellence are put to the test.

In the current model, due to the "*global pandemic of Covid-19*", an event of this magnitude transforms the current paradigm from its foundations, creating a "new normality". Some of us doubt that this is by chance, since obviously in an unconscious capitalism, one of its variables at play is still the "servility and control" of the masses for its functioning. Precisely one of the reasons why there is no "conscious capitalism" is because of mass media propaganda in the service of governments. Therefore, the population, unless there is eventually a critical mass that wakes up, the paradigm does not change, but only mutates.

With these statements, we intend to arrive at the fact that implementing a conscious enterprise will only become a reality when it is perceived to be profitable for its creators. If this conviction does not exist, the prevailing paradigm prevents the creation of a different reality in society and in the market. Today, precisely because of the weariness and saturation of an unsustainable model like the one we have now, financially, socially and politically, with sufficient evidence of corruption and dehumanization, workers are looking for greater transcendence and purpose in their actions and are developing a more human perspective of companies where the barriers that lead us to separate who we are at work and outside work are removed, where we connect with the aspirations and needs of different stakeholders.

Because of this human perspective, organizations with a purpose that connects with their stakeholders and that is demonstrated, day by day, by the example and behavior of their managers and employees, obtain better financial results. Every self-respecting organization seeks to add value to its internal and external environment, to solve an existing problem in the market and to provide a solution to it, through excellence. This is what Edward Freeman, of the University of Virginia, makes clear in his book *Strategic Management: A Stakeholder Approach*. Professionals want to work in them; suppliers want to collaborate with them; consumers do not hesitate to buy their products or services; investors bet on these businesses, and this becomes an inertia that demonstrates the profitability of these companies.

Conscious companies are those that align their vision, culture and strategy, and therefore obtain up to three times better results, according to the article *The Hidden Value of Organizational Health -and How to Capture It* by McKinsey, elaborated between 2003 and 2011 from 800 organisations and more than 1.5 million employees. We also find in *Firms of Endearment*, the authors of a study in which they compare the financial performance of companies based on a holistic model with companies in the S&P 500 index over a 15-year period. The research, in general terms, highlights that conscious organizations obtain better results with lower risk than the rest of the companies.

Basically, the characteristics that define this profitability can be summarized in the following points:

Optimizing risk management. By being proactive with stakeholders, responsible companies are better able to meet challenges: motivated and engaged employees, consumers who share the organization's values, or investors who are satisfied with the results.

Reduced costs and greater efficiency in business processes. The increased concern of companies for all aspects of their operations helps them to spend their resources on what is important to the company's purpose.

Improving competitiveness in the market by introducing differentiating features. Conscious companies do not just sell a product or service, but also bring values such as supporting local communities, creating great places to work, or respecting the environment, among others, which become another reason for the customer to buy there, rather than from the competition.

Boosting a positive brand image and enhancing the company's *reputation* by sharing the wealth generated with all stakeholders.

Increased employee satisfaction, which in turn generates higher staff productivity.

Reduced risk of customer boycotts.

Strong relationships with stakeholders.

Conscious leaders

According to JV Crum III, author of Conscious Millionaire: Grow Your Business By Making a Difference, a conscious leader acts under the following parameters:

The benefits of collaboration versus competition. Better results can be obtained by joining forces than by opting for confrontation. The conscious leader looks for a win-win formula for all stakeholders.

Ability to see opportunities. For conscious leaders, the market is full of possibilities if you are attentive to what society needs. This ties in with the previous idea, as conscious companies can find their own market niche, without having to compete with the rest.

Capacity for alignment versus alienation. Subjugation only leads to fear and distrust, so those who feel dominated will flee when given the opportunity. Conscious leadership, on the other hand, spreads its belief in the company's purpose to all stakeholders, so that they too share its vision and goals, working to achieve them with loyalty and passion.

Holistic analysis of reality. Managers who follow a holistic postulate, "*the trees do not prevent them from seeing the forest*", as is popularly said. They have the ability to perceive reality as a whole, which contributes to their decisions being more accurate and beneficial for all the organization's groups and objectives.

Ability to adapt to change. The future does not generate bewilderment or anguish in conscious leaders, who see challenges as new avenues for improvement based on acquired experience. Their optimistic attitude and focus on conflict resolution give them great abilities to adapt to new scenarios. In times of paradigm shift such as we are experiencing in 2020, leaders with this ability will flourish, becoming the new "*gurus*" to follow.

Assumption of the importance of teamwork: what would they be without their employees? For conscious leaders, the company's human capital is a fundamental part of the company's success and, therefore, they develop a close bond with employees, based on respect, recognition, and trust.

According to previous analysis, the model that comes closest to a holistic model would be the *Economy for the Common Good*, a proposal for an economic and social model, centered on people and which is a lever as a paradigm shift. It is a concrete, possible, viable and applicable alternative for companies and society in general. Today, CBE is an international movement that has launched an open and participatory process, which is continuously growing, and which seeks socio-economic changes at a local and global level. CBE became visible with the publication of Christian Felber's book "Economy of the Common Good" in Austria in August 2010.

This new economic and social paradigm promotes the Product of the Common Good indicator, to overcome the limitations of the current GDP. In the case of companies, the CBE promotes that success should be measured by the *Common Good Balance Sheet*, because the traditional Financial Balance Sheet of companies does not reliably inform us if the profit has been obtained by destroying jobs, with deplorable working conditions, or by indiscriminately exploiting the environment, producing materials or services that do not contribute anything to the common good.

According to the official EBC website, the type of organisations that follow the holistic model of the Economy for the Common Good include Universities, Educational Centres, Companies, Associations, etc.: https://economiadelbiencomun.org/tag/asociacion-federal-espanola/

Typically, this is a Common Good Balance Sheet, like an audit of the Common Good Matrix, and a number of points are awarded, totaling 1000. The Common Good Matrix is the heart of this model, which can be considered a holistic model. One of the main value propositions of the Economy of the Common Good model is that it is an open model, where all the tools necessary to do the Common Good Balance Sheet are available to organizations that wish to do so.

Organizations decide on a voluntary basis how far they want to go in using these tools. They can do the Balance Sheet with their own resources, ask the accredited Consultants of the Federal Association for support to do the Full Balance Sheet, the reduced version or simply use these tools as a guide for improvement plans on the social and environmental impact of their projects. This is an example of a matrix made by a Valencian City Council.

As we can see, it is a holistic model for any business organization in which the WHOLE is considered:

On the one hand, it considers all the parties involved in their interaction, from users, funders, suppliers, etc.

On the other hand, what level of involvement they have in terms of solidarity, social justice, sustainability, transparency, participation.

Analysis of the Holistic Model in an organisation at the present time

Nowadays, most business organizations, faced with changing situations such as those we are experiencing in an environment of globalization, are forced to look for new strategic models. When a depersonalized model like the one we are perceiving in the market, and everything so technician, the consumer feels more comfortable and secure with more human models. To be more precise, we are now of developing Artificial Intelligence, which, even the most expert, do not know how a technification of their lives will affect human beings.

Equipping organizations with the tools to be more productive and efficient is a premise that we all accept and agree on. But what will happen if Technology and Artificial Intelligence replace human beings, and this paradigm ends up imposing itself, dehumanizing organizations?

I have my serious doubts that the Establishment really wants everyone to have access to the same tools and information, or that everyone on this planet lives in a natural ecosystem without pollution, with unpolluted air and blending in with nature.

On the contrary. There are small countries like Switzerland, some Northern European countries, which do have these privileges. And we see that in a situation of "population control", for whatever reason, societies act differently. There is clear evidence that AI will provide much more control over the population (China has already implemented the points-based programme), if you take advantage of all the information that will be available, as we provide and feedback more and more data. Therefore, more than ever, a *strict code of ethics* must be followed and validated by countries, so that technology is used for the good of society.

All this sounds like utopia and big words, but there are examples of citizens, even, who are already mobilizing in this direction. I will quote someone I know personally, Jaime Garrido, collaborator of Cuarto Milenio, the architect "Jaigar", who has created the "strict ethics" in the construction sector, a code of ethics for a sector that has not respected good practices in times of overcrowding: https://jaigarr.net/es/paradigma-de-la-etica-estricta/

Nowadays it is true that it is utopian to implement a *strict holistic model*, as there should be a global paradigm shift in terms of the fact that the population is not prepared to accept this level of ethical demands. One of the premises that any citizen must analyze is what excellence means, what it means to improve and evolve in a business organization and in society in general.

We question something that is on everyone's lips at the moment, technology: should it be open, can those who possess it take advantage of it, and in fact they do, to implement control over the citizenry for the sake of false security and data protection? *The great challenge we face today with AI is undoubtedly the degree to which this technology can be implemented for the evolution of society or the control of a few and coexist while continuing to evolve as human beings.*

What do we mean by conscious entrepreneurship?

The concept of conscious entrepreneurship is based on the vision of the holistic paradigm, which in its principle's states that the purpose of such a model, of a complete vision of reality, is to evolve consciousness; it also originates from the concept of "Conscious Capitalism". (Aburdene, P. 2006). Conscious Capitalism is a term coined by Patricia Aburdene in her book Mega Trends 2010, *which refers to the emergence of a capitalism with a human face, based on spirituality, ethical, which realizes the ideal of a market oriented to the evolution of consciousness.*

We can define a conscious entrepreneur as an individual who uses his or her inner spiritual potential to create one or more successful enterprises with the characteristics of conscious capitalism, such as developing within a framework of ethics and respect for the natural, social, political, and cultural environment.

To achieve an experience in a holistic model, it is vital that education emphasizes the holistic formation of the human being, with the essential aim of happiness. Marci Shimoff says that there are "*two barriers that stand between us and happiness*", and that these barriers *are fear and anxiety,* produced by the attachment to everything that gives us pleasure and we fear losing; by the aversion to everything that causes us pain and as such we reject it, but also the ignorance of our true human nature, which is happiness and pure love, is the cause of our suffering. This is the essence of where holism comes from.

Business organizations originating from this holistic perspective will be projects that integrate the search for the common good, as well as the benefit of the entrepreneur himself, those businesses will hopefully be part of the life purpose of each of their creators and their full realization as human beings, who seek true happiness and sustainability in their environment, as expressed by the investor Malcolm Forbes: "*Business arose to produce happiness, not to accumulate millions*" (Berenstein, M., 2008. p.13).

According to Jörg Zittlau, an entrepreneur whose "most striking characteristic of the modern leader is that, unlike his predecessor, he does not have his capital invested in the company, but he has a lot of ideas about how to invest it. He has no leather armchairs, but an orthopedic office stool. He does not enslave the employees he manages but integrates them into the decision-making processes. He is performance-oriented and willing to give up.

He doesn't know what it's like to hoard money, and instead is passionate about investing money. The manager doesn't rely on previous successes but is constantly on the lookout for novelty and creativity. (Zittlau, J. 2007, p. 14). We see a model with a holistic view of leading an organization, with no attachment to anything material, although at the same time his creativity will generate material abundance and prosperity wherever he leads.

We need to radically change the educational paradigm and established beliefs in society, as well as the purpose of a Business Organization. The new paradigm in the formation of human beings needs to be based on a Holistic vision, an educational vision that integrates the formation of future entrepreneurial business leaders with a mission and a deep spiritual vision in their own lives and their companies, as it is well known that business is the reality of human life, which is why it is necessary to negotiate and have economic activities, with which to generate wealth for the welfare of diverse cultures and societies.

Conscious entrepreneurs must prepare themselves in a disciplined way in the practices of meditation or reflection on the purposes that lead them to lead an organization, so that they understand their contribution to society through the companies they lead, so that as a result they can be truly full and happy beings. This would be the primary purpose of a holistic model, a new paradigm that provides human beings with wisdom and full knowledge of our capabilities.

This is also the purpose of the middle path proposed by the Eightfold Noble Path, to support the formation of conscious entrepreneurs, and implicit in it of course is "having enough to eat and wear; enough money to live comfortably is a worthy goal, and the desire to do something for oneself can indeed become a powerful, life-enriching energy" (Inamori, K. 2009, p. 3).

Among all these goals in the outer life of the human being there is one that is directly related to full happiness, for which Inamori says: "*there is one thing you must not leave behind: your spirit. What have we done with our lives?*" (Inamori, K. 2009, p. 3).

In order to achieve a transformation of the future conscious entrepreneur, an integrative proposal is required, from education to questioning all the beliefs that society has so far integrated at a collective level. The proposal based on the holistic paradigm is based on a new scheme of values that will produce transformational changes. As a conclusion and according to Gallegos Nava, R. 2001.p. 30-3, we must transform the following aspects, and we will have more conscious entrepreneurs:

- ✓ Shifting from the myth of progress to sustainable balance
- ✓ Shift from competition to economic cooperation
- ✓ Changing the desacralization of nature, realizing that our planet is a living being
- ✓ Shift from a policy of winners-losers to a policy of entrepreneurship with a win-win-win-win vision.
- ✓ Long-term program change. Conscious entrepreneurs create businesses that last.
- ✓ Shift from bureaucratized and inflexible institutions to participatory organizations
- ✓ Shift from consumerism to responsible consumption
- ✓ Shift from quantitative to qualitative priorities
- ✓ Shift from the scientific as absolute truth to various forms of knowledge as relative truths
- ✓ Change from an education system for industry to an education model for life Change from fragmented awareness to awareness of the whole

Trying to explain a holistic model in the business world is not an easy task. Many entrepreneurs do not even understand the holistic concept of creating a business organization or taking a project forward with this perspective. Furthermore, there is a belief in the collective unconscious, due to the established economic system of animal competitiveness that exists, that applying a holistic model is not compatible with the benefits and sustainability of a business.

It is to be aware and responsible for its capacity and actions in the market/society, solving a problem for a certain population group, applying its full potential, thus generating prosperity and mutual benefit. For this purpose, a model based on the principles of Social Responsibility is applied, adding a holistic commitment within this framework, implementing the procedure of a CSR Report. The *Holistic Social Responsibility Plan* has been created on the basis of several concepts that are emphasized, such as: awareness, commitment, training/experience and transparency.

Integrating the Laws of the Kybalion in Entrepreneurship

Mentalism: How the entrepreneur's mindset can influence business success and how to apply the law of mentalism to set goals and visualize success. The Law of Mentalism, the first of the Seven Hermetic Laws of the Kybalion, states that "*All is Mind; the universe is mental*".

This law is essential to understanding how holistic entrepreneurship relates to the teachings of the Kybalion.

The Mind of the Entrepreneur: The Law of Mentalism teaches us that the mind is the basis of all creation. In entrepreneurship, this means that a business idea first arises in the mind of the entrepreneur. The clarity of that idea, its originality and its viability are directly related to the quality of the mind that conceives it. An entrepreneur who understands this law understands that the quality of his or her thinking and imagination will directly influence the success of his or her business.

Visualization and Creation: The Law of Mentalism also implies that everything that exists in the material world first had to be conceived in the mind. Holistic entrepreneurs practice creative visualization. They imagine themselves and their businesses succeeding even before it happens in physical reality. This practice not only motivates them to move forward, but also creates a thought form that has the power to materialize in the physical world.

Creating an Entrepreneurial Culture: The entrepreneurial mindset is contagious. If a business leader has a positive, growth-oriented mindset, this will be reflected in the company's culture. A positive mental approach can inspire employees, encourage innovation, and overcome challenges. A thorough understanding of the Law of Mindset means that an entrepreneur can influence the collective mindset of his or her team and thus the overall success of the business.

The Power of Focus: The Law of Mentalism also teaches that the mind is in constant motion. For entrepreneurs, this means that they must learn to focus their minds on the ideas and goals they want to achieve.

Constant and focused attention on business goals creates a mental energy that can lead to success. However, a scattered and unfocused mind can lead to erratic decisions and lack of direction in business.

Law of Mentalism and Empathy: Understanding that "All is Mind" also implies deep empathy. Holistic entrepreneurs who understand this law can better connect with their customers and employees. They can understand the needs and desires of others at a deeper level, enabling them to develop products and services that truly solve problems and meet market needs.

In short, the Kybalion's Law of Mentalism reminds us that thought is the precursor to all manifestation in the physical world. For holistic entrepreneurs, this means cultivating a positive, growth-focused mindset, visualizing success, focusing on goals and practicing empathy. By applying these principles, entrepreneurs can create thriving and meaningful businesses that not only generate financial returns, but also contribute positively to the world around them.

2. Correspondence: Exploration of the interconnectedness between different aspects of the business, such as the relationship between the customer and the product, and how understanding these correspondences can improve operations.

The Law of Correspondence states that "*as above, so below; as below, so above*". This hermetic law implies that there is a correspondence and connection between the different planes of existence, from the highest and spiritual to the lowest and material. In the context of entrepreneurship, this law can be profoundly enlightening and practical.

Business Vision and Reality: In the world of entrepreneurship, this law suggests that the vision an entrepreneur has for his or her business (above) must be matched with the reality and day-to-day operations of the business (below). This means that the values, mission and culture that are defined in the boardroom should be reflected in the way employees interact with customers, in the quality of products or services and in the overall reputation of the company.

Relationship with Customers: The Law of Correspondence also implies that the way a company treats its customers (below) directly affects the customers' perception of the company (above). A business approach that shows respect, empathy and care for customers will correspond to a loyal and satisfied clientele. On the other hand, negligent or disinterested treatment will correspond to loss of customers and a negative reputation.

Internal Coherence: Within a company, coherence between top management, middle management and grassroots employees is essential. Clear communication and an organizational structure that corresponds to the company's goals and values ensure a harmonious flow of work. A disconnect between these levels will lead to confusion, lack of direction and ultimately business failure.

Product/Service Development: The law of correspondence also applies to product or service development. If a company seeks to create something valuable and useful for its customers (above), it must ensure that the final product or service meets the expectations and needs of the market (below). The correspondence between the initial idea and the final product is crucial for long-term success.

Innovation and Adaptation: In an ever-changing business world, companies must adapt and evolve to remain relevant. The law of correspondence implies that strategies and business models (above) must match market demands and trends (below). Companies that can successfully adapt to these changes will remain relevant and successful over time.

Organizational Culture: The culture an organization (above), including its values, ethics and way of doing business, should correspond to the way employees behave in their work environment (below). A company culture that fosters creativity, collaboration and accountability will correspond to engaged and productive employees.

In conclusion, the Kybalion's Law of Correspondence teaches us that there is a deep connection between different aspects of entrepreneurship, from business vision and culture to the way we interact with customers and develop products. Entrepreneurs aware of this law can align their actions and decisions with their higher goals, creating businesses that thrive not only materially, but also in terms of meaning and contribution to the world around them.

Vibration: How energetic vibrations in the business environment can influence productivity and the working environment, and how to create a positive vibration in the business.

The Kybalion Law of Vibration states that "*nothing is at rest; everything moves; everything vibrates*". This Hermetic law teaches us that everything in the universe is in constant motion and vibration, including our thoughts and emotions. Related to the business world, this law has profound implications:

Business Energy: Every company has its own energy and vibration. This energy is reflected in the way employees interact with each other, in how customers perceive the company and in the overall atmosphere of the workplace. An entrepreneur aware of the Law of Vibration understands that positive energy and a proactive attitude can raise the vibration of the company, creating an environment conducive to creativity, innovation and productivity.

Emotions and Business Decisions: The emotions of leaders and employees have a direct impact on business decisions. Negative emotions, such as fear or indecision, can lead to impulsive or poorly informed decisions. A business leader aware of the Law of Vibration knows that maintaining positive emotions, such as confidence and determination, can influence strategic decision making, promoting sustainable business growth.

Market Resonance: Businesses that understand the Law of Vibration can tune themselves to the needs and desires of the marketplace. By understanding the vibrations of the market, entrepreneurs can tailor their products, services and marketing strategies to resonate with customers. This involves not only being aware of trends, but also capturing the "emotional vibe" of the target audience and responding authentically and empathetically.

Positive Organizational Culture: The Law of Vibration also manifests itself in organizational culture. Companies that promote a positive vibe attract and retain talented and engaged employees. A culture based on trust, respect and collaboration resonates with employees, which in turn translates into more positive customer service and strong business relationships.

Innovation and Creativity: The positive, energetic vibe in a company is a breeding ground for innovation and creativity. Teams working in a high vibrational environment are inspired and motivated to generate new ideas and find creative solutions to business challenges.

Entrepreneurial Attitude: An individual's entrepreneurial attitude, including their level of confidence and willingness to take risks, is closely related to their energetic vibration. An entrepreneur who radiates confidence and positivity will attract positive opportunities and partnerships, which will contribute to the growth and success of their business.

In short, the Kybalion Law of Vibration reminds us that energy and vibration are fundamental in the business world. Entrepreneurs who understand and apply this law can raise the vibration of their businesses, creating an environment conducive to growth, innovation, and long-term success. By maintaining a positive vibration in all aspects of business, from internal interactions to customer relationships, companies can flourish on a deeper and more meaningful level.

4. Polarity: The importance of balance in business, how to recognize and manage polarities within a company to maintain a harmonious flow.

The Kybalion's Law of Polarity states that "*everything is dual; everything has poles; everything has its pair of opposites; like and unlike are the same; opposites are identical in nature, but different in degree; extremes touch; all truths are half-truths, all paradoxes can be reconciled*". In the business context, this law offers profound and practical lessons:

Recognizing the Dualities of Entrepreneurship: In the business world, dualities are inevitable. There is success and failure, growth and decline, opportunities, and challenges. Wise entrepreneurs understand that these dualities are inherent to the entrepreneurial process and that the key lies in finding a dynamic balance. Accepting that success and failure are two sides of the same coin allows entrepreneurs to better manage the fluctuations in their entrepreneurial journey.

Transforming Challenges into Opportunities: The Law of Polarity teaches that opposites are identical in nature, but different in degree. Business challenges can be seen as opportunities in disguise. For example, an economic crisis can be seen as an obstacle, but also as an opportunity to innovate and diversify. Entrepreneurs can take advantage of this law to transform seemingly negative situations into learning and growth experiences.

Work-Life Balance: Polarity also manifests itself in the entrepreneur's life, where dedication to work must be balanced with attention to personal and family life. Too much focus on work can lead to burnout and neglect of personal relationships, while too much attention to personal life can negatively affect business productivity. Finding the right balance is essential for both personal and business well-being.

Understanding Emotions and Relationships: Interpersonal relationships are also subject to the Law of Polarity. Human emotions oscillate between positive and negative. Entrepreneurs who understand this law can manage conflicts and tensions in the team, knowing that human relationships can be transformed from negative to positive with the right approach and understanding.

Integrate Different Perspectives: The best business decisions often arise from the integration of different views and approaches. Polarity manifests itself in the diverse opinions and approaches within a team. Smart entrepreneurs can reconcile these differences and find solutions that integrate opposites harmoniously, harnessing the power of diversity in the decision-making process.

Develop Entrepreneurial Resilience: Resilience is fundamental in the business world. Entrepreneurs who understand the Law of Polarity develop greater resilience by accepting and adapting to change. By understanding that adverse situations are temporary and can be transformed into opportunities, entrepreneurs can maintain a positive mindset even in difficult times.

In short, the Kybalion's Law of Polarity offers valuable lessons for entrepreneurs. By embracing dualities and learning to balance opposites, entrepreneurs can make wiser decisions, better manage challenges and maintain a positive and resilient outlook. By applying these lessons, entrepreneurs can build strong, sustainable businesses that thrive even in changing and challenging business environments.

5. Rhythm: How to recognize natural cycles in business and adapt to them to seize opportunities and overcome challenges.

The Kybalion's Law of Rhythm states that "*everything flows, in and out; everything has its tides; everything rises and falls; everything moves like a pendulum*". In the business context, this law offers valuable lessons about the cyclical nature of business and how entrepreneurs can adapt and thrive in an ever-changing world:

Understanding Business Cycles:

The Law of Rhythm reminds us that businesses have natural cycles of boom and bust. Wise entrepreneurs recognize these cycles and prepare for the tough times during the good times. They understand that successes are temporary and that challenges will pass. This understanding allows them to remain calm and make informed decisions during market fluctuations.

Adaptation to Market Changes:

The business market is constantly changing. Trends, customer demands, and technology evolve in cycles. Successful entrepreneurs are those who can adapt to the changing pace of the market. They can identify when the time is right to launch a new product or service and when an existing product needs to be withdrawn or reinvented.

Seizing Opportunities:

Pace also means opportunities come and go. Astute entrepreneurs can recognize the right time to expand their business, enter new markets or form strategic partnerships. Learning to synchronize business actions with the pace of the market can lead to significant growth opportunities.

Maintaining Persistence and Discipline: The Law of Rhythm also relates to persistence. Successful entrepreneurs understand that success often does not come immediately, but after a period of constant effort and dedication. Maintaining a steady pace of work and discipline, even when results are slow in coming, is critical to achieving long-term business goals.

Avoid Impulsive Decisions: The pendulum of the Law of Rhythm implies that things can change at any time. Wise entrepreneurs avoid making impulsive decisions based on temporary situations. Instead of reacting impulsively to market fluctuations, they make decisions based on a thorough understanding of long-term trends and how the rhythm of the market will develop in the future.

Foster a Culture of Adaptability: Companies that thrive are those that can adjust their internal pace to match the pace of the market. Fostering a culture of adaptability and flexibility within the company enables employees to respond nimbly to change and stay attuned to changing customer needs.

In short, the Kybalion's Law of Rhythm underscores the importance of understanding and synchronizing with the natural cycles of the market and the business world. Entrepreneurs who understand this law can anticipate change, adapt with agility, and make informed decisions, enabling them to navigate the ups and downs of the business world with grace and lasting success.

Holistic Business Approaches

Conscious Management: How practicing conscious management can improve decision-making and relationships with employees and customers.

Case Study: Whole Foods Market - Focus on Conscious Management

Background: Whole Foods Market is a supermarket chain focused on natural and organic foods. They have pioneered conscious management by incorporating sustainable practices, workplace equity and a focus on community into their business model.

How Whole Foods Applies Conscious Management:

Responsible Products: Whole Foods is committed to selling products that are ecologically responsible and of high quality, supporting local and sustainable producers.

Organizational Culture: The company creates a positive and equitable work environment, offering fair wages and benefits for employees. They have implemented wellness and personal development programs for their staff.

Community Involvement: Whole Foods is actively involved in local communities through donation and volunteer programs, supporting charities and education projects.

Practical Advice for Entrepreneurs:

Clarity on Values: Clearly define your company's core values and ensure they are aligned with conscious management, including sustainability and equity.

1. **Transparency and Honesty:** Be transparent about your business practices and communicate openly about your conscious efforts to your employees and customers.
2. **Employee Involvement:** Involve your employees in decision making and listen to their ideas and concerns. Foster a culture of trust and collaboration.
3. **Social Responsibility:** Actively contribute to your local community through donations, volunteer programs and other corporate social responsibility initiatives.
4. **Work-Life Balance:** Encourage a healthy work-life balance for your employees. Consider offering flexible hours and support for mental and physical well-being.

Case Study: Patagonia - Integrating Conscious Values in the Company

Background: Patagonia, the renowned outdoor clothing, and equipment company, is known for its commitment to environmental and social responsibility. They have applied conscious management principles in their business model.

How Patagonia Applies Conscious Management:

Environmental Sustainability: Patagonia uses recycled materials and green manufacturing practices to minimize their environmental impact. They also donate part of their profits to support environmental causes.

Employee Welfare: The company offers flexible working hours, welfare and personal development programs for its employees, showing a strong commitment to their well-being and development.

Social Activism: Patagonia uses its platform to raise awareness about social and environmental issues. They have launched campaigns and donated large sums of money to support various causes.

Practical Advice for Entrepreneurs:

1. **Genuine Commitment:** Conscious management must be a genuine commitment, not just a marketing strategy. Make sure your actions are backed by authenticity and passion.
2. **Responsible Innovation:** Investigate and adopt innovative and sustainable practices in your supply chain, packaging and daily operations.
3. **Education and Awareness:** Educate your employees and customers about your conscious efforts. Awareness and understanding can encourage support and participation.
4. **Product Life Cycle:** Consider the full life cycle of your products, from production to disposal. Design products that are durable and encourage recycling practices.
5. **Impact Measurement:** Establish metrics to measure your impact on the community and the environment. These metrics can help you improve and show your progress over time.

By studying these case studies and following the practical advice, entrepreneurs can apply conscious management in their businesses, creating not only profitable, but also socially and environmentally responsible enterprises.

Economics for the Common Good: Introduction to the economic model that values not only financial success, but also social and ecological well-being.

Case Study: Trivium Packaging - Integrating the Common Good Economy

Background: Trivium Packaging is a global metal packaging company. They have adopted principles of the Economy for the Common Good (EBC) in their operations to create a positive impact on society and the environment.

How Trivium Packaging Applies the Economics of the Common Good:

Transparency and Accountability: Trivium Packaging has implemented transparency measures in its operations, allowing for greater visibility into its supply chain and production practices.

Sustainability: The company is committed to reducing its carbon footprint and using sustainable materials in its packaging. They have also implemented recycling and reuse programmes.

Fairness and Solidarity: Trivium Packaging maintains fair labour practices and has implemented programs to support local communities in the regions where they operate.

Practical Advice for Entrepreneurs:

1. **Impact Assessment:** Conduct a thorough assessment of your company's impact on society and the environment. Identify areas for improvement and set clear and measurable goals.
2. **Stakeholder Engagement:** Involve employees, customers and suppliers in the decision-making process. Listens to their concerns and perspectives to create a more equitable and supportive company.

3. **Non-Financial Value:** Consider the non-financial value of your shares. This includes the positive social and environmental impact your company can generate. Measure and communicate these values transparently.
4. **Partnerships:** Collaborate with other companies and organizations that share the values of the Economy for the Common Good. Collaboration can amplify positive impact and create beneficial synergies.
5. **Education and Awareness: Educate** your employees and customers about the importance of the Economy for the Common Good. Awareness and understanding are key to creating meaningful change.

Case Study: Organic Valley - Farmers' Collective Applying the Principles of the Common Good Economy

Background: Organic Valley is an agricultural cooperative of organic farmers in the United States. They have adopted the principles of the Common Good Economy to create a sustainable and equitable agricultural model.

How Organic Valley Applies the Economics of the Common Good:

Equity and Solidarity: Organic Valley operates as a cooperative, which means that member farmers have a voice in decisions and share the benefits equally.

Sustainability: The cooperative focuses on sustainable agricultural practices, including organic farming, rotational grazing, and soil conservation.

Transparency and Accountability: Organic Valley is transparent about its operations and agricultural practices, allowing consumers to know where its products come from.

Practical Advice for Entrepreneurs:

1. **Cooperative Model:** Consider establishing a cooperative model in your industry. Participation and equity are fundamental to the Economy for the Common Good.
2. **Certifications and Sustainable Practices:** Obtain certifications that support your sustainable practices. Make sure your operations are aligned with ecological and ethical standards.
3. **Consumer Education:** Educate your customers about the importance of choosing products and services that follow ethical and sustainable principles. Consumer awareness can drive change in the marketplace.
4. **Community Development:** Contribute to the development of the local communities where you operate. Supports projects and programs that improve the quality of life and promote equity and solidarity.

These case studies illustrate how companies can apply the principles of the Economy for the Common Good to create more equitable, sustainable, and socially responsible business models.

By adopting these principles and following the practical advice, entrepreneurs can contribute to positive change in the business world and society at large.

Social Entrepreneurship: How entrepreneurs can address social and environmental problems while running a profitable business.

Case Study: TOMS - One for One Model

Background: TOMS is a well-known footwear and accessories brand that has adopted a "One for One" business model. For every product they sell, they donate a product or service to people in need, such as shoes, glasses or medical services.

How TOMS Applies Social Entrepreneurship:

Direct Donation: For every pair of shoes sold, TOMS donates a pair of shoes to a child in need. They have expanded their model to include eyeglass donations and support for eye surgery programs.

Measurable Impact: TOMS tracks and publishes the impact of its donations. Customers can see the exact number of products donated and which communities have been reached.

Awareness campaigns: The company not only donates products, but also raises awareness about the issues they address, such as poverty and lack of access to healthcare.

Practical Advice for Entrepreneurs:

1. **Identify a Key Need:** Find an important social need that your product or service can address. Identify a cause that resonates with both you and your customers.
2. **Transparent Donation Model:** Make sure your donation model is transparent and easy for customers to understand. Transparency increases consumer confidence in your brand.
3. **Long-term impact:** Consider the long-term impact of your donations. Assess how your contributions can create sustainable change in communities in need.

Case Study: Grameen Bank - Microfinance for Empowerment

Background: Grameen Bank, founded by Muhammad Yunus, is a pioneer in the field of microfinance. They provide small loans to low-income people, especially women, to start or expand small businesses.

How Grameen Bank Applies Social Entrepreneurship:

Financial Access: Grameen Bank provides access to finance for people who would not have access to traditional loans. This allows them to start small businesses and improve their living conditions.

Promoting Women's Empowerment: Most beneficiaries are women. Grameen Bank recognizes the transformative impact of women's economic empowerment in communities.

Poverty Reduction: By providing finance to small entrepreneurs, Grameen Bank contributes significantly to poverty reduction in the areas where it operates.

Practical Advice for Entrepreneurs:

1. **Long-term commitment:** Empowerment through microfinance takes time. Make a long-term commitment to see significant results.
2. **Additional support:** Offer not only financing, but also training and support to entrepreneurs. Business knowledge and skills are as important as money.
3. **Impact Monitoring:** Track the impact of your program. Assess how loans have improved the lives of beneficiaries and use this information to improve your services.

These case studies highlight how companies and entrepreneurs can apply social entrepreneurship to address social and economic problems, while building sustainable and ethical businesses. The principles of transparency, long-term commitment and impact measurement are key to success in this field.

B-Corp: Explanation of certified B-Corporations that balance social and environmental purpose with business success.

Case Study: Patagonia - Leader in Corporate Responsibility

Background: Patagonia is an outdoor clothing and equipment company that has been a B Corporation since 2012. The company is known for its strong commitment to environmental sustainability and social responsibility.

How Patagonia Applies the B-Corp Model:

Environmental sustainability: Patagonia has adopted sustainable practices throughout its supply chain. They use recycled materials, reduce waste and are activists in the fight against climate change.

Community Involvement: The company donates 1% of its sales to environmental organizations and is involved in numerous community initiatives and conservation programs.

Product Responsibility: Patagonia promotes the durability and repairability of its products to reduce waste and encourage a conscious consumer approach.

Practical Advice for Entrepreneurs:

1. **Sustainable Innovation:** Research and adopt sustainable practices in your supply chain and operations. Innovation is key to finding effective environmental solutions.
2. **Transparency:** Be transparent about your business practices and your efforts to improve social and environmental impact. Transparency builds trust.
3. **Advocacy and Activism:** Actively engage on social and environmental issues. Customers value companies that use their influence to do good in the world.

Case Study: Ben & Jerry's - Ice Cream with a Purpose

Background: Ben & Jerry's is a famous ice cream company that has been part of the B Corporation movement since 2012. They are known for their focus on social and environmental justice.

How Ben & Jerry's Applies the B-Corp Model:

Sustainability and Fair Trade: They use sustainable and ethically sourced ingredients. They have worked on programmes to support farmers and their communities.

Social Advocacy: Ben & Jerry's has been involved in numerous social justice campaigns and is known for its advocacy for civil rights and equality.

Participatory Governance: The company practices a form of participatory governance that involves employees and stakeholders in key decisions.

Practical Advice for Entrepreneurs:

1. **Develop a Clear Mission:** Define a mission that integrates both business objectives and social and environmental impacts. The mission should be the core of your business.
2. **Employee Involvement:** Involve your employees in social and environmental initiatives. Creative ideas and internal support are essential for success.
3. **Measurable Impact:** Establish metrics to measure your impact on the community, environment and other social aspects. Measurement allows you to assess your progress and continuously improve.

These case studies illustrate how B-Corp companies, such as Patagonia and Ben & Jerry's, are using their business models to create a positive impact on the world while maintaining sound and ethical business operations. These examples demonstrate that it is possible to be both socially and environmentally responsible and successful in business at the same time.

Conclusion

A recapitulation of the principles of holistic entrepreneurship and how the laws of the Kybalion can guide entrepreneurs towards a more conscious and balanced approach to business.

An invitation to readers to apply these principles in their own ventures and contribute to positive change in the business world.

It is important to note that the teachings of the Kybalion are philosophical and spiritual, and their application in the business world may vary according to individual interpretation and perspective. However, there are entrepreneurs and business leaders who have adopted holistic and spiritual principles in their business practices. Here are some examples of entrepreneurs who have applied concepts related to the laws of the Kybalion in their businesses:

1. Ray Dalio (Bridgewater Associates): Ray Dalio, founder of Bridgewater Associates, one of the world's largest hedge funds, is known for applying philosophical principles in his business management.

In his book "Principles", Dalio presents a set of principles that guide his decision-making, including the idea that everything is connected and that recurring patterns can be identified and used to make more informed business decisions.

2. Arianna Huffington (The Huffington Post, Thrive Global): Arianna Huffington, founder of The Huffington Post and Thrive Global, is an advocate for wellness and the importance of work-life balance. She has spoken about the importance of meditation and sleep in business performance, concepts that align with holistic teachings related to vibration and balance.

3. **Steve Jobs (Apple Inc.):** Although there is no direct evidence that Jobs studied the teachings of the Kybalion, his focus on simplicity and elegant design in Apple products reflects the airtight idea that "as above, so below". Jobs applied this principle by integrating aesthetics and functionality in Apple products, creating a harmonious user experience.

4. Richard Branson (Virgin Group): Richard Branson, founder of the Virgin Group, has spoken about the importance of maintaining a balanced approach to life and business. He has applied principles of resilience and adaptability in his business approach, which relates to the Kybalion's Law of Rhythm.

5. Oprah Winfrey (Harpo Productions, OWN Network): Oprah Winfrey has been outspoken about her practice of mindfulness and the importance of intuition in decision-making. These concepts align with Kybalion teachings related to mind and vibration.

It is important to note that these examples illustrate how some business leaders have integrated philosophical and spiritual principles into their business approaches. How they interpret and apply these teachings may vary, and each entrepreneur may have his or her own unique perspective on how to apply holistic principles in the business world.

Case Study: Patagonia - Integrating Holistic Values in the Enterprise

Background: Patagonia is an outdoor clothing and equipment company known for their environmentally and socially conscious approach. They have applied holistic principles in their business to create a positive impact on the world while being commercially successful.

How Patagonia Applies Holistic Principles:

1. **Environmental Sustainability:** Patagonia has led the industry in sustainability. They have used recycled materials in their products and have advocated responsible manufacturing practices.
2. **Social Responsibility:** The company donates 1% of its sales to environmental conservation organisations and has led campaigns to protect the environment and natural spaces.

3. **Employee Care:** Patagonia cares for the well-being of its employees, offering benefits such as time off for outdoor activities and mental wellness programmes.

Practical Advice for Entrepreneurs:

1. **Define your Values:** Identify your company's core values. These values should guide all business decisions and actions.
2. **Integration into Company Culture:** Make sure that holistic values are integrated into your company culture. This includes the way you treat your employees, customers and the environment.
3. **Transparency and Communication:** Be transparent about your holistic practices and efforts. Communicate these initiatives to your customers and employees to build trust.
4. **Sustainable Innovation:** Research and adopt sustainable and innovative business practices. This may include green technologies, responsible manufacturing practices and eco-friendly packaging.
5. **Community Partnership: Collaborate** with local and community organizations to make a positive contribution to the society in which you operate. This may include education programmes, donations or volunteer activities.

Case Study: Ben & Jerry's - Social Engagement and Corporate Responsibility

Background: Ben & Jerry's is a famous ice cream company known for its social and political commitment. They have integrated holistic principles into their business from the beginning.

How Ben & Jerry's Applies Holistic Principles:

1. **Fair Trade:** The company is committed to sourcing ingredients through fair trade, ensuring that farmers receive a fair wage for their products.
2. **Environmental sustainability:** Ben & Jerry's has implemented sustainable practices in its supply chain, including renewable energy and waste reduction.
3. **Social activism:** They have used their platform to advocate for important social issues such as equal marriage and climate change.

Practical Advice for Entrepreneurs:

1. **Authentic Engagement:** If you are going to advocate for social causes, make sure that the engagement is authentic and aligns with your company's values.
2. **Employee Involvement:** Involve your employees in social and environmental initiatives. They can suggest ideas and actively contribute to the company's efforts.
3. **Measurement and Transparency:** Measure and disclose your impact. Use metrics to evaluate your social and environmental efforts and share these results with your stakeholders.
4. **Creative Campaigns:** Develop creative campaigns that engage customers. This may include events, special promotions, or fundraising programs for charities.
5. **Persistence:** Social and environmental responsibility is not just a trend; it is a long-term commitment. Remain persistent in your efforts and keep looking for ways to improve and make a positive impact.

By studying and applying these case studies and practical tips, entrepreneurs can find inspiration and guidance to apply holistic principles in their own businesses, thus contributing to a more conscious and sustainable business world.

This book has analyzed the current state of the Holistic concept: what it consists of what are its characteristics, what types of studies of this kind exist, what has been its evolution, what are the advantages of its use in a business organization, what challenges an entrepreneur faces in a new global social and economic paradigm. And, above all, in the new social and economic paradigm that is coming? Given the pandemics and the economic and social crisis we are experiencing, would a holistic system be a viable alternative to solve this problem?

Its potential for application to the business processes involved in what is known as Total Quality has also been analyzed. To this end, the holistic concept is approached as a 360-degree global vision for the understanding and vision of all the processes involved in an organization, inside and outside it. Likewise, as entrepreneurs, hopefully we apply holistic to excellence and ethical commitment in an organization. The processes in an organization are not unidirectional, on the contrary, Excellence in Knowledge Management is analyzed back and forth, that everything influences, from within the organization, from what vision the entrepreneur/founder has, and how it affects the environment, and how the environment affects the entrepreneur and the organization that has been created.

Finally, this book has been the subject of a proposal on the skills and mission that every entrepreneur should have in a changing and global environment such as the current situation, where technology and the human coexist on unequal terms, since everything is becoming more and more technological, and everything can have a rapid impact on the stakeholders of a Business Organization with a social commitment and for the common good of the economy and society.

ABOUT THE AUTHOR

This book is written by an entrepreneur with more than 25 years of experience, I have always pursued independence and my best self through entrepreneurship. It is a consciously chosen path, with its ups and downs and joys, it is a life choice. I am 52 years old, and I am still thinking about new projects, I think until I leave this world. I hope this book inspires you as I have been inspired by others. Thank you for being part of this journey of entrepreneurship. www.escueladelemprendedor.com